REASONS

FOR A

NEW EDITION

OF

SHAKESPEARE'S WORKS,

AMS PRESS

NEW YORK

REASONS

FOR A

NEW EDITION

OF

SHAKESPEARE'S WORKS,

CONTAINING NOTICES OF THE

DEFECTS OF FORMER IMPRESSIONS,

AND POINTING OUT

THE LATELY ACQUIRED MEANS OF ILLUSTRATING THE PLAYS,

POEMS, AND BIOGRAPHY OF THE POET.

———

BY

J. PAYNE COLLIER, ESQ. F.S.A.

AUTHOR OF THE HISTORY OF

ENGLISH DRAMATIC POETRY AND THE STAGE, &c.

———

SECOND EDITION, WITH ADDITIONS.

———

LONDON:

WHITTAKER & CO. AVE MARIA LANE.

———

1842.

Library of Congress Cataloging in Publication Data

Collier, John Payne, 1789-1883.
    Reasons for a new edition of Shakespeare's works.

    1. Shakespeare, William, 1564-1616--Criticism,
Textual.   I. Title.
PR3071.C6 1973   822.3'3   79-113586

Reprinted from the edition of 1842, London
First AMS edition published in 1973
Manufactured in the United States of America

AMS PRESS INC.
NEW YORK, N. Y.   10003

ADVERTISEMENT.

THE want of a Library Edition of Shakespeare's Works, comprising the latest discoveries and elucidations made by the continued efforts of celebrated Antiquaries and Commentators, has induced the Publishers to avail themselves of Mr. Collier's knowledge, ability, and zeal on this subject, in order to present the Public with as perfect an Edition, more especially as regards the text of the Plays and Poems, as can be given, and in such a form and size as shall render it at once available to the scholar and the general reader.

To prove the necessity of such an undertaking, they have requested Mr. Collier to draw up the ensuing statement.

The Work will be comprised in Eight handsome Demy Octavo Volumes, printed in a large type, in the best manner, on a suitable paper; and will be issued in volumes periodically, commencing on the 1st of February, 1842. A Specimen-page is appended[1].

The Publishers would feel particularly obliged by purchasers notifying, at their earliest convenience, to their respective booksellers their intention to take the work, as the number printed will be regulated accordingly.

WHITTAKER AND CO.

Ave Maria Lane,
London, January, 1842.

---

[1] This Specimen was originally selected by the Publishers before it was corrected by the Editor.

To several subjects: heaven hath my empty words,
Whilst my invention, hearing not my tongue,
Anchors on Isabel: Heaven in my mouth,
As if I did but only chew his name,
And in my heart the strong and swelling evil
Of my conception. The state, whereon I studied,
Is like a good thing, being often read,
Grown sear'd and tedious [1]; yea, my gravity,
Wherein (let no man hear me) I take pride,
Could I, with boot, change for an idle plume,
Which the air beats for vain. O place! O form!
How often dost thou with thy case, thy habit,
Wrench awe from fools, and tie the wiser souls
To thy false seeming! Blood, thou art blood:
Let's write good angel on the devil's horn,
'Tis not the devil's crest.

Enter Servant.

How now, who's there?
   Serv.   One Isabel, a sister,
Desires access to you.
   Ang.   Teach her the way.   [*Exit Serv.*
O heavens!
Why does my blood thus muster to my heart;
Making both it unable for itself,
And dispossessing all my other parts
Of necessary fitness?
So play the foolish throngs with one that swoons;
Come all to help him, and so stop the air
By which he should revive: and even so
The general, subject to a well-wish'd king,
Quit their own part, and in obsequious fondness
Crowd to his presence, where their untaught love

---

[1] *Grown* sear'd *and tedious;*] Warburton suggested *seared* for "feared" or
"fear'd," as it stands in most copies of the first folio: that belonging to Lord
Francis Egerton has it *sear'd,* as if the letter *s* had been substituted for *f* as the
sheet was going through the press. We need not, therefore, doubt as to the
adoption of *sear'd* instead of "fear'd."

REASONS,

&c.

THE object of the following pages is to answer the question—" Why is it proposed to publish a new edition of the Works of Shakespeare ?"

In an undertaking of the kind, no point is of so much importance as to settle the text of the author; and notwithstanding the pains bestowed upon the language of Shakespeare, from the days of Rowe to the present time, I shall be able to show that his Editors have done much that they ought not to have attempted, as well as left undone much that they ought to have accomplished. They have been guilty of serious offences of omission as well as of commission; and this may be said with all due respect for their labours and their learning, for the industry with which they have at times prosecuted their inquiries, and for the acuteness and knowledge many of them have displayed in the investigation of disputed questions. It is of course impossible to bestow too great pains on ascertaining and fixing the true reading of Shakespeare; and minute and patient accuracy of comparison of the old copies, quarto and folio, printed in his lifetime or soon afterwards, is indispensable. This is the most sacred part of the duty of an Editor, and the absence of that minute and patient accuracy is unpardonable in any person who undertakes the task of producing an impression of the works of such an Author.

Means of settling the Text.   Let us examine briefly, in the first place, the means for settling the text that remain to us, and then, the manner in which those means have been hitherto employed.

Manuscripts.   Dramatic pieces in manuscript by Ben Jonson, Beaumont and Fletcher, Massinger, Middleton, and others, are in existence [1]; but it is a remarkable fact, that not a single written fragment of any of the Plays of Shakespeare has come down to us, with the exception of a few passages in some unprinted poetical miscellanies. It was very much the custom with our ancestors, in the reigns of Elizabeth and James I., to keep common-place books, in which they entered anecdotes, observations, or passages from works which fell in their way. Considering the number of such collections, known to be extant, it is singular that so few quotations should have been inserted in them

[1] I refer to the autograph productions of Ben Jonson among the Royal MSS. in the British Museum ; to the copy of the " Humorous Lieutenant" (under the title of " Demetrius and Enanthe") published by my friend the Rev. A. Dyce ; to the " Parliament of Love," printed by Gifford, among the works of Massinger ; to Middleton's " Witch," &c. In addition to these, many anonymous plays of the same era have been preserved, besides fragments by celebrated dramatists. In the " Memoirs of Edward Alleyn," printed for the Shakespeare Society, I have inserted a considerable portion of Robert Greene's " Orlando Furioso," and I have in my possession a small part of Marlowe's " Massacre at Paris," possibly in the handwriting of the poet.

from plays, and especially from plays by Shakespeare. One of these, forming rather a rare exception to the general rule, is now before me, and it contains extracts from several of our great dramatist's productions for the stage, anterior to the year 1600, but none afterwards, although the dates interspersed in the volume (of some 500 closely written pages) extend from about 1590 to the breaking out of the civil wars. It rarely happens that the title of the play is given, but "Richard II." and "The Merchant of Venice" are mentioned, and about five other dramas are quoted. Whether the writer of this common-place book (who appears to have been either a barrister or an attorney) employed the printed copies, resorted to manuscript authorities, or only recorded striking passages which he heard at the theatres, it is not easy to decide; but even these brief extracts, never exceeding five lines, now and then throw light upon difficult and doubtful expressions. In general, collections of this kind consist solely of undramatic poems, or citations from them, and of these several have devolved into my hands; and, as will be seen hereafter, one of them very importantly illustrates the minor productions of Shakespeare. It comprises sonnets by Sir Philip Sidney, poems by Daniel and Drayton, Ben Jonson's ballad "From Oberon in Fairy-land" (with additions), and other pieces; but more especially, as regards my purpose, some manuscript copies at full length of poems contained in Shakespeare's "Passionate Pilgrim," originally published in 1599, and subsequently in 1612.

These are sources of information, as regards the genuine text of Shakespeare, to which former Editors either did not resort at all, or very sparingly employed; and by availing myself of them, as largely as the nature of the case will allow, it will be seen that something has been accomplished for the illustration of the productions of our great dramatist.

Printed authorities.

I shall also with the most plodding diligence go over every line, word, and letter of each play or poem, in order to be sure that the new edition corresponds with the ancient copies, as far as they are to be followed, and that no syllable is passed over or omitted that can be corrected or recovered. Upon this task I have more or less been employed for many years, as I was able to procure copies of the original editions ; but of late I have enjoyed facilities for the purpose of going through the plays again, and of completing my undertaking, such as, I may confidently assert, no other Editor ever possessed.

Duke of Devonshire's Collection.

The moment it was mentioned to the Duke of Devonshire (to whose kindness in other respects I owe much) that I had engaged to produce so important a work as a new edition of Shakespeare, and that frequent reference to his Grace's matchless dramatic library would be of essential service, the Duke at once insisted that I should take home with me every early edition of Shakespeare in his library, that I might be able to finish my collations at leisure, and under all possible advantages. Such an excess of confidence I was not prepared to expect, even from the Duke of Devonshire; but of course I was most happy to accept so extraordinary a favour. When I state that his Grace's collection includes all the first editions of Shakespeare's dramas, and most of the later impressions prior to the Restoration,—that it embraces the inestimable and *unique* first "Hamlet," of 1603,—the first "Romeo and Juliet," of 1597,—the first "Richard II." and "Richard III.," of the same year,—the three "Lears," of 1608, — "The Merry Wives of Windsor," of 1602,—the "Othello" of 1622, and many others, which, if brought to the hammer, would produce a sum of money, the amount of which it is difficult in these times to calculate, the reader will be able in some degree to estimate this remarkable act of liberality. From his Grace also I have obtained the loan of his folio editions of the Works of Shakespeare in 1623, 1632, 1664, and 1685.

But the Duke of Devonshire is not the only nobleman to whom I am indebted in this respect. Lord Francis Egerton would have required no example of the kind to prompt him to do any thing in his power to aid me in this design; but it so happened that I had directed my earliest application to the Duke of Devonshire, and I could not refrain from making Lord Francis Egerton acquainted with the fact and its result. When I resorted to the noble possessor of the Bridgewater Library, I was

Lord Francis Egerton's Library.

met with a proposal that I should be furnished from thence with all the plays, poems, or tracts, that would contribute to my purpose. Thus I obtained the *unique* "Titus Andronicus" of 1600,—many of the first and subsequent editions of other pieces by our great poet,—the *unique* drama of " Love and Fortune," 1589, and various other plays, poems, and pamphlets, intrinsically of great curiosity, and to me of most essential importance. Early impressions of plays, even of the same edition, not unfrequently differ, improvements having been made, and errors corrected while they were going through the press [1]; and it was

---

[1] This point has never been at all attended to, and the difficulty in some instances of procuring more than a single copy of a play, has led to the repetition of important mistakes. " Love's Labours Lost " was first printed in 1598, and the copies of the Duke of Devonshire and of Lord Francis Egerton vary in one place singularly. The passage occurs in act iv. sc. 3, where Biron, before he is himself detected, thus reproaches the King, Longaville, and Dumain, with having fallen in love :—

> " When shall you see me write a thing in rhyme,
>   Or groan for *Joan* ?"

This is as the passage has been uniformly printed, " Joan " in the 4to, 1598, belonging to Lord Francis Egerton, and in others used by former editors, being spelt *Ione.* Nobody seems to have suspected an error, but that there was one cannot be disputed ; for in the copy of the same edition belonging to the Duke of Devonshire, instead of " groan for Ione " we have " groan for *Love*," with a capital, as if to prevent the blunder (detected while the play was going through the press) from being repeated. The fact is, that the compositor misread the *l* in " love " for a capital *I*, and the *u* (then almost invariably employed instead of *v*) for an *n*, and printed " Ione " instead of " loue."

Another, even more remarkable, instance occurs in " The Merchant of Venice," of which there are two 4to editions in 1600, one by Heyes and the other by Roberts. The Duke of Devonshire and Lord Francis Egerton have copies of the edition by Heyes, and they vary importantly near the com-

therefore highly useful to me thus to have an opportunity of collating one copy against the other[1]. Lord Francis Egerton was also kind enough to add to the obligation, by lending me his folios of 1623 and 1632, the first being more than ordinarily interesting on account of certain early manuscript corrections in a few of the plays, which will put an end to doubts on some passages of the original text, and will most satisfactorily illustrate and explain others not hitherto well understood.

Perhaps, before I proceed farther, it may be well MS. corrections in a folio of 1623. to adduce a few proofs of the interest and value of the folio of 1623, belonging to Lord Francis Egerton, in this particular. It should be observed preliminarily that the volume is not perfect, and that some

mencement of act iv. In that of the Duke of Devonshire two lines are thus given :—

> " Well use question with the wolf,
> The ewe bleat for the lamb ;"

which is unintelligible. The defect must have been discovered while the play was going through the press ; and in the copy of the identical edition, the property of Lord F. Egerton, the passage is made to run correctly as follows :—

> " You may as well use question with the wolf,
> Why he hath made the ewe bleat for the lamb ;"

and so the passage stands in the 4to by Roberts, which the editors of the folio of 1623 evidently never saw.

[1] Of course the dramatic collections in the British Museum, and at Oxford and Cambridge, have been open to me as to others, and whenever occasion has arisen, it will be found that they have been duly consulted ; but the extraordinary aids I have obtained in the two instances above referred to, and the assistance I have derived from the libraries of my friends, have rendered a resort to public establishments less frequently necessary. Many years ago I completed a collation of the text of Shakespeare with such of the original quarto editions of his plays as are preserved in the British Museum.

deficient leaves have been supplied by manuscript. This manuscript is not older than the end of the seventeenth or beginning of the eighteenth century, and as it was made from an impression of the second folio of 1632, it is in itself of no worth; but certain corrections, in the margin of the printed portion of the folio, are probably as old as the reign of Charles I. Whether they were merely conjectural, or were made from original manuscripts of the plays, to which the individual might have had access, it is not perhaps possible to ascertain. As has been stated, these verbal, and sometimes literal, annotations are only found in a few of the plays in the commencement of the volume; and from what follows, it will be a matter of deep regret that the corrector of the text carried his labours no farther.

" All's Well that ends Well."   Our earliest instances shall be taken from " All's Well that ends Well," and these alone would be sufficient to establish the excellence of the proposed emendations. In the dialogue between the King of France and Helena, (act ii. sc. 1.) where she is endeavouring to persuade him to use her remedy, she concludes one of her speeches, according to the wording of the folio of 1623, with these lines:—

> " Oft expectation fails, and most oft there
> Where most it promises; and oft it hits
> Where hope is coldest and despair most *shifts*."

Now, it is very clear that "shifts" cannot be right: Pope, and all subsequent editors, conjecturally

substituted *sits;* but the MS. corrector of Lord
Francis Egerton's folio has written *fits* in the
margin; and " 'fits," for *befits,* was probably the
word Shakespeare wrote, the transcriber or printer
mistaking the *f* for a long *s,* then invariably used
at the beginning of words [1].

Another instance of a similar error, arising precisely from the same cause, is pointed out by the MS.
corrector near the end of the same play, (act v. sc. 3.)
where the King (following the exact reading of the
first folio) thus addresses Bertram :

> " I wonder, sir, sir, wives are monsters to you,
>   And that you fly them as you swear them lordship,
>   Yet you desire to marry."

The repetition of " sir" in the first line must be an
error, and modern editors have substituted *since,*
which would answer the purpose, if it were the true
word : the true word is " for," which was often used
in Shakespeare's time instead of *because* or *since :*
the compositor mistook the *f* for a long *s,* and the *o,*
perhaps imperfectly written, for *i.* The line should
stand—

> " I wonder, sir, *for* wives are monsters to you," &c.

and so it is made to run by the individual who set

---

[1] In Shakespeare's Sonnets (cxx.) we meet with " fits " for *befits* in the
line,
> " The humble salve which wounded bosoms *fits;*"

and the instance is the more apposite, because it rhymes with " hits," as in
the quotation from " All's Well that Ends Well."

right a few of the mistakes in the first folio belonging
to the Bridgewater library.

But there is a still happier emendation in the
same play, which not a single editor ever hit upon ;
yet it is so obvious, that the moment it is mentioned,
it will seem wonderful how so many learned and
ingenious men could have overlooked it. It occurs in
the last scene of act ii. after the King has compelled
Bertram to marry Helena against his will, and Bertram has resolved to fly from her for ever before the
consummation. Bertram's speech to Parolles stands
in the following manner, as originally printed in the
folio of 1623 :—

> " I have writ my letters, casketed my treasure,
>   Given order for our horses ; and to-night,
>   When I should take possession of the bride,
>   And ere I do begin."

Thus the passage passed through the four early
folio editions, and all others from Rowe downwards,
excepting that in some of the modern impressions,
those who superintended them, not understanding the
concluding hemistich above inserted, printed it as if
Bertram had not finished his sentence, and was inter-
rupted by Parolles,

> " And ere I do begin————"

when the whole alteration that is required, to make
the sense perfect and intelligible, is a single letter,
and that single letter is written in the margin of the

folio of 1623, the property of Lord Francis Egerton.
If we read

> " *E*nd ere I do begin."

all that is necessary is accomplished, and the evident
meaning is that Bertram, escaping from the wife he
has just been compelled to marry, resolves to *end* the
union *ere he begins it:*

> "I have writ my letters, casketed my treasure,
> Given order for our horses; and to-night,
> When I should take possession of the bride,
> *End ere I do begin.*"

It must be acknowledged that this is a very easy
and happy emendation, which does not admit of a
moment's doubt or dispute.

Nearly the same may be said of two of the changes
in " The Winter's Tale" proposed by the same authority. In act i. sc. 2. Hermione tells Leontes, as we
find it in all the editions,

> —— —— ——" Yet, good deed, Leontes,
> I love thee not a jar o' the clock behind
> What lady she her lord."

which reads very like nonsense, although no attempt
has been made to correct a decided error. If we
read *should*, instead of " she," in the third line, the
whole difficulty is removed; and probably in the
MS. from which the first folio was printed " should"
was written with an abbreviation, which might easily
be misread by the compositor. The MS. corrector
of Lord Francis Egerton's folio has substituted
should for " she " in the margin. Another, more than

" Winter's Tale."

B

plausible, alteration was made by the same hand in a
later part of the same play, act v. sc. 1. A gentle-
man describes the beauty of the Princess whom
Florizel has brought with him ; and Paulina, apostro-
phising Hermione, exclaims—

—————————————" O, Hermione!
As every present time doth boast itself
Above a better gone, so must thy grave
Give way to what 's seen now.''

Edwards (author of the " Canons of Criticism") remarks on this passage that " thy grave" means *thy
beauties ;* but the truth seems to be that the printer
mistook a letter in the word " grave." In Lord F.
Egerton's folio, *grace* is substituted in MS. for
" grave," and " grace" was constantly used by our
ancestors as synonymous with " beauty."

It would be easy to carry this subject farther, and
to adduce other instances, all tending to establish
what a service would have been rendered to Shakespeare, if the early possessor of this copy of the folio
of 1623, instead of confining his corrections to a few
of the plays which appeared in that edition for the
first time, had gone through the whole collection,
including those originally printed in quarto and afterwards reprinted in the folio. Only eighteen out of
six-and-thirty plays had appeared in quarto before the
publication of the folio in 1623 ; so that precisely the
same number were new to the press when Heminge
and Condell published their edition. These last the
player-editors must have derived from MSS. belong-

ing to the company of the King's servants, to which they were still attached.

Readers in general are not at all aware of the Careless-ness of col-lation. nonsense they have, in many cases, been accustomed to receive as the genuine text of Shakespeare; and from a comparison of some of the plays, as they stand in the first folio, with modern copies, I shall now proceed to establish, how carelessly former editors have executed the necessary, but mechanical work of collation. I shall not refer to dramas of which there are several old quarto editions, which would have required exact examination, and might possibly have somewhat distracted the attention of the commentators, but to those printed, for the first time, in the folio of 1623; where an editor, as far as regards collation, had no more to do than to take care that his text follows that of the single ancient impression under his eye, with only occasional re-ference to the second folio, of 1632. And here I Folio of 1632, its value. may take occasion to remark, that although the folio of 1632 is not to be considered a decisive authority, it is by no means to be so slightly treated, as Ma-lone was disposed to do, in opposition to Steevens: Steevens was certainly willing to rely too much upon it; but, although it is not uniformly well corrected, and although a few of the plays appear to have entirely escaped attention, it is indisputable that it was not a mere reprint, left to the mercy of com-positors, but that some editorial care was exercised in the production of considerable portions of it.

Its changes are nevertheless not to be invariably adopted; and although the supervisor of it might possibly have resorted to then existing manuscripts, I do not think it probable that he did so, nor do I perceive sufficient evidence of the fact to warrant the degree of confidence in his emendations they would in that case deserve.

Two Gentlemen of Verona.

With this remark I will cite a few passages from " The Two Gentlemen of Verona," to prove that the modern editors of Shakespeare strangely neglected the duty they undertook, as far as respects furnishing an authentic text, supported by the best authority to which they could refer—the folio of 1623. The modern text is taken as it is found in the edition in 21 vols. 8vo., which the late Mr. Boswell saw through the press, and which contains Malone's latest corrections and contributions, besides the notes of Pope, Theobald, Warburton, Johnson, Steevens, Reed, and other commentators, during considerably more than a century.

In act i. sc. 2, of " The Two Gentlemen of Verona," Julia asks her maid, Lucetta, her opinion of her various suitors; and first,

" What think'st thou of the fair Sir Eglamour ?"

To which Lucetta replies, according to the folio of 1623,

" As of a knight well-spoken, neat and fine."

How is this line printed in Malone's Shakespeare by Boswell?   Thus:—

" As *our* knight, well-spoken, neat and fine."

In the same scene, on the re-entry of Lucetta, Julia inquires,

" Is it *near* dinner time ?"

and Lucetta's answer completes the line,

———————" I would it were."

In Malone's Shakespeare, by Boswell, the word " near" is omitted in Julia's question, by which the metre is destroyed; and the omission is the more extraordinary, because Boswell added a note of his own, to inform the reader, that " Is it" was printed " Is 't" in the folio; but he did not carry his attention even to the very next word, or he must have seen that it was wanting, even if his ear did not make him acquainted with the deficiency.

Passing over mere misprints, of which a formidable list might be furnished from this very play, the following striking errors of a different kind in a small part of a single page (iv. 102), are not to be forgiven.

" You would *then* have them always play but one thing."

The adverb in italic is an interpolation, without the slightest reason assigned, and as the passage is only prose, no excuse could be found in the requirements of the metre [1].   In fact, in this scene, some

---

[1] The excuse of the improvement of the metre (though we ought to be far from wishing for any such *improvements*,) may however be made for the unwarranted insertion of the same adverb in a line of " The Taming of the Shrew," act i. sc. 1.

" In brief, *then*, sir, sith it your pleasure is," &c.

If commentators and verbal critics were to be allowed on all occasions to

passages meant for colloquial verse, just above the level of ordinary speaking, have been printed by Malone as prose; such, for instance, as Julia's answer to the line above quoted, which ought to be regulated thus:—

> " I would always have one play but one thing.
> But, Host, doth this Sir Proteus, that we talk on,
> Often resort unto this gentlewoman ?"

A few lines farther we meet with a careless transposition, which I should not have noticed, but for the other defects in the same passage : the observation of Proteus,

> " Sir Thurio, fear not you, I will so plead,"

was allowed by Boswell to stand,

> " Sir Thurio, fear *you not*, I will so plead[1]."

Again, on the re-appearance of Silvia at her

---

amend in their own way what they might consider the defective metre of Shakespeare, they would generally make strange work of it. Steevens was the boldest experimenter of this class, although his ear was notoriously most exceptionable. It is not the province of an editor to attempt to *improve* Shakespeare.

[1] In the following instance of the same kind from " The Taming of the Shrew," the transposition would seem to have been wilful :—

> " This will I do, and this will I advise you,"

as if, because " will I" occurred in the first clause of the sentence, it was necessary that it should be repeated in the second. It is printed, " and this *I will* advise you" in the folio ; and perhaps the very reason which induced Malone to make the change (without any notice that he had done so,) was the very reason why Shakespeare wrote the contrary. Where no alteration is absolutely necessary, we are apt to consider the poet the best judge of the mode in which he will express himself.

window, Proteus, in the old copy of 1623, addresses
her—

> " Madam, good even to your ladyship ;"

which is printed by Malone—

> " Madam, good *evening* to your ladyship,"

avoiding the authorised and refined term Shakespeare purposely employed, and giving an air of
familiarity to the salutation, inconsistent with the
relative positions of the parties to the dialogue.
These errors (not one of which is countenanced even
by the text of the second folio) are all included
within a space of nineteen lines ; and on the very
next page (103), we meet with a passage which is
rendered pure nonsense by the substitution of one
word for another. Silvia is reproaching Proteus with
injuring his friend by making persevering love to
her, and she asks—

> ———————— " and art thou not ashamed
> To wrong him with thy importunacy ?"

Thus it stands in the first and in all the folio
editions ; yet in Malone's Shakespeare, by Boswell,
the preposition has been absurdly changed, and the
passage is thus given :—

> ——————— " and art thou not ashamed
> To wrong him *of* thy importunacy ?"

A form of expression neither authorised by the
original text, nor by the customary mode of writing

in the time of Shakespeare. No blunder of the kind can be deemed a trifle, (even if it did not make the passage unintelligible,) where an editor professes to fix the genuine reading of such an author; and when in a subsequent scene of the same act (act iv. sc. 4), we meet with "all men's judgment," misprinted for "all men's judgments," both substantives having been correctly and consistently written by Shakespeare in the plural, all lovers of our great dramatist ought to be offended.

This system of blundering (for it may be said to amount almost to a system) is kept up to the very last scene of "The Two Gentlemen of Verona," where Valentine, addressing the Duke, observes, as the lines appear in the folio of 1623,—

> " And as we walk along, I dare be bold,
>   With our discourse, to make your grace to smile."

In the copy of the play in the edition in 21 vols. 8vo, revised by Boswell and containing Malone's latest corrections, we find *alone* substituted for "along," just as if two people could walk alone, and as if the Duke and Valentine would not be surrounded by the other prominent characters in the drama, besides being attended by the ducal train.

So far with regard to some of the errors in " The Two Gentlemen of Verona;" but the case of that play is by no means singular, and in others the mistakes are hardly to be accounted for, excepting

by supposing culpable carelessness combined with
remarkable ignorance (of which of course we do not,
in the ordinary sense of the word, accuse the commentators), in order to disfigure the text of Shakespeare[1]. In one drama, " The Taming of the Shrew," a Taming of
the Shrew.
whole line has been omitted, and Boswell (who has
been ostentatious of his collations, pointing them out
in separate notes at the foot of the page) did not
detect the deficiency. It cannot indeed be said that
the sense is absolutely incomplete without this missing
line, but still it is necessary to the full meaning of the
author, as will be evident when we quote the passage
as we find it in the folio of 1623, where the play

[1] Now and then, changes are made which could not be accidental, and
for which there is not the slightest warrant by supposing the meaning of
the poet to have been misrepresented by the old printers. The alteration
in the following lines from " The Winter's Tale," (act. v. sc. 1) seems
merely wanton, and it runs through all the modern impressions. Paulina
would not have Leontes marry again, and Dion, in reply, urges her to pity
the State, and to call to mind the necessity of continuing the succession in
the family of Leontes :—

> ——————— " If you would not so,
> You pity not the State, nor the remembrance
> Of his most sovereign name ; consider little
> What dangers, by his highness' fail of issue,
> May drop upon his kingdom."

Nothing can be plainer, but all the modern editions substitute *dame* for
" name," (as it stands in the folio) and thus absolutely contradict the
poet's meaning. Shakespeare would hardly have made Dion advert to the
fate of Hermione, at the moment when he was urging another marriage
upon the king. Moreover, in the folio of 1623, and in the three others, as
if to prevent the possibility of mistake, " Name " is printed with a capital
letter. This was therefore a wilful corruption of the text, without any
notice that a variation had been made from the old and authentic reading
of the play.

(as well as the others we have noticed) was for the first time printed. It is in act iv. sc. 3, (as the divisions are commonly marked, though it is the beginning of the fourth act in the original copy,) where Katherine is intreating Grumio to give her something to eat :—

> " Beggars that come unto my father's door
> Upon entreaty have a present alms,
> If not, elsewhere they meet with charity ;
> But I, who never knew how to entreat,
> *Nor never needed that I should entreat,*
> Am starv'd for meat, &c."

The line printed in Italic is the line omitted, and in what way it made its escape from the text we cannot conjecture ; but the fact that it was omitted must put an end to confidence in such an edition, and proves that Boswell (to say nothing of Malone) performed his duty of collation with almost criminal inattention [1].

---

[1] I do not complain of misprints in plays not assigned to Shakespeare, but included by Boswell in the 21 vols. ; such for instance as " The True Tragedie of Richard the Third." (vol. xix.) Not only are lines left out, but exits and entrances are omitted, and other more or less important . variations from the old copy are innumerable.

It is but justice to state, that the passage in " The Taming of the Shrew" is correctly printed in Mr. Knight's " Pictorial Shakspere," and I add with pleasure my testimony to the improvements he has made in the text of previous editions, by restoring some of the readings of the first folio. I may take this opportunity, also, of expressing my sense of the obligations Mr. Knight has, in other respects, conferred upon the readers of Shakespeare, both by the originality of some of his views, and by the ingenuity and ability with which he has enforced and illustrated them. He has pointed out a line in " Hamlet," which was left out by Reed in 1803, but it is restored in Malone's Shakespeare by Boswell, vol. vii. p. 241.

We might produce various instances from the same comedy, where words have been foisted upon Shakespeare without notice, or omitted without reason ; but one striking proof of extreme carelessness we cannot refrain from pointing out : it occurs at the close of act iv., where Hortensio says—

> " Well, Petruchio, this has put me in heart.
> Have to my widow ; and if she be froward,
> Then hast thou taught Hortensio to be untoward."

The three lines are given as above in the several folio editions, excepting that " be," in the second line, is omitted in the first edition, and supplied by the second ; but in Malone's Shakespeare by Boswell, not only " has" is altered to *hath*, (a matter of comparatively small moment, though still an unjustifiable liberty,) but " froward " is made *forward*, the sense of which is directly opposite to that of Shakespeare, while it destroys the intended rhyme, which, without any other aid, ought to have led to the detection of the error.

The point of infidelity to the text having been thus completely made out, by reference only to a few plays of which there are no quarto editions, it would be tedious, as well as useless, to dwell longer on that subject.

Nor is punctuation, in an undertaking of this kind, a matter merely trivial, especially when non-attention to it not only obscures, but sometimes entirely perverts, the sense of a passage. In this respect very flagrant errors have been committed ;

Punctuation.

but it is a topic to which we shall advert very briefly, and only introduce one or two passages from the modern edition, in order to show the nature, rather than the extent of our complaint. Here, of course, we do not object that the ancient authorities have been deserted, because the matter seems usually to have been left to our old printers, and they were notoriously either heedless or incompetent. The consequence has been frequent blunders and confusion; but we must say that in some instances it would have rendered Shakespeare more intelligible, if the pointing in his day, or shortly afterwards, had been adopted. Of the correctness of this statement we may be permitted to bring forward a solitary example, out of many. It is from "The Winter's Tale," act i. sc. 2, where Polixenes and Camillo are conversing about the evil designs of Leontes, and the former says, as we find it in the first folio,

> ———————————————"Camillo,
> As you are certainly a gentleman, thereto
> Clerk-like, experienc'd, which no less adorns
> Our gentry," &c.

This very perspicuous quotation is rendered utter nonsense by the false punctuation employed in Malone's Shakespeare by Boswell, where it reads as follows :

> ———————————"Camillo,——
> As you are certainly a gentleman thereto ;
> Clerk-like, experienc'd, which no less adorns
> Our gentry," &c.

In the same way, what can be the meaning of the mark of interrogation, where, in " Twelfth Night" (act i. sc. 5), Viola having asked, " The honourable lady of the house, which is she ?" Olivia replies,

" Speak to me ; I shall answer for her ?"

This is an answer not a question, though it is immediately followed by " Your will ?" The old printers did not commit this error. It is very true that in many cases these mistakes correct themselves; but even then, they are awkward disfigurements, checking the smooth progress of perusal, to say nothing of the manner in which they may destroy the meaning of the author. No difficulty could be found in adducing hundreds of places to which this observation will apply : they are to be pointed out on almost every page.

A few remarks regarding the metre of Shakespeare, and the manner in which it has been preserved or injured by his later editors, is all that will be necessary on this head. It must be admitted that some of them, especially Steevens, have taken most capricious liberties, and have shown that though they might be very exact counters of syllables, they had very bad ears for the harmony of Shakespeare's rhythm. There is no doubt, that defects of this kind found their way into the old editions, but we are not at liberty to insert or omit words, merely because we may imagine that lines would run better with them or without them. I am firmly persuaded that many passages, now considered defective, were

Shakespeare's Metre.

purposely left so by the poet, with a view of giving
variety, and of avoiding that weighty and tedious
monotony observable in the works of all his immediate predecessors, with 'the solitary exception of
Marlowe. Hence, not only Shakespeare's lines of
eight, but those of twelve or more syllables, of which
there are frequent examples : the first some of his
commentators would lengthen by needless expletives,
and the last they would shorten by cutting out what
they are pleased to consider unimportant epithets—
as if a poet, of whom it has been said that he never
used a word for which a better could be substituted,
could employ unimportant epithets. Supposing a
line to be objectionable in either respect, it is as
easy for the reader to amend it, as for the commentator : to make such changes at all is highly censura-
ble, but to do so without notice is utterly inexcusable.

What is often to be complained of is, that the
editors of Shakespeare have not availed themselves
of the ordinary means in their power for rendering
his verse such as we may presume he intended it to
be. Thus they have sometimes injuriously deviated
from the mode in which the metre is regulated in
the old copies of the plays, particularly in the first
folio. I take leave to say, after having gone through
every line of it, that this volume, notwithstanding
the cavils of some of the commentators, is more correctly printed than any other dramatic production of
the time, with the exception perhaps of the folio
edition of Ben Jonson's Works in 1616, the passage

of which, through the press, there is good reason to believe he superintended [1]. Let any body compare the typographical execution of the folio of 1623 with that of any plays printed or reprinted between the years 1600 and 1630, and they will be aware of the laudable pains that must have been bestowed upon it. The present is not the place for entering farther into this point, and I will only take the opportunity of introducing one specimen of the manner in which the beauty of the genuine text of Shakespeare, as given in the folio of 1623, has been disfigured by modern attempts at emendation: this has not been

[1] Some people have expressed surprise, if Ben Jonson were really the editor of the folio of his Works in 1616, that he did not include in it " The Case is altered," which was printed with his name on the title-page in 1609. Hence it might be conjectured, against the strongest internal evidence, that the comedy was not in truth his, and the supposition is apparently supported by the fact, that the Duke of Devonshire has in his library a copy of " The Case is altered," without Ben Jonson's name in any part of it. However, it is, I think, quite certain, that Ben Jonson only meant to include in his folio, plays of which he was the sole author, and that he excluded " The Case is altered," because some other dramatist (as may indeed be gathered from diversity of style,) aided him in its composition. He is known to have written various plays in partnership with Dekker, Porter, Chettle, and others, at the end of the reign of Elizabeth, and in the beginning of that of her successor ; but, as he had not the sole authorship, nor probably the sole property in them, he omitted them when he printed his collected Works. May not the same reason have induced the player-editors of the folio Shakespeare in 1623, to leave out various pieces in which he had been more or less concerned, and which he wrote in conjunction with other poets, according to the constant practice of the time ? It is supposed with considerable plausibility that Shakespeare wrote part of Ben Jonson's " Sejanus," as originally played at the Globe in 1603 ; but, when the latter printed it as his own, he re-wrote the whole of what had been contributed by a " second pen," and apologised for omitting what came from " so happy a genius."

accomplished by absolutely adding or taking away anything, but by the non-observance of elisions and abbreviations, necessary to the metre, and frequent in the old copy. We take our specimen from " All's well that ends well," act ii. sc. 1—the opening of a speech by Helena to the king of France, respecting her father:

> " The rather will I spare my praises towards him ;
> Knowing him is enough. On's bed of death,
> Many receipts he gave me ; chiefly one,
> Which, as the dearest issue of his practice,
> And of his old experience th' only darling,
> He bade me store up."

Here we find no defective line, but all run regularly and musically, exactly as they are inserted in the first folio; but in the modern editions, we find the verse rendered lame and imperfect, by printing words at length which were meant to be elided: thus, " On's bed of death," is given " *On his* bed of death," and " th' only darling," is lengthened out into " *the only* darling," to the great offence of an acute and sensitive ear[1].

To show how little attention has been paid to

[1] It has been suggested to me that these elisions ought not to be made manifest by the printer, but left to the ear, as in Italian and Spanish : in the first place, however, in English we have fewer vowels, and they do not always melt into each other with facility ; and in the next, a reader, not accustomed to elide words without notice, by means of an apostrophe, would often have to correct his own mistakes of perusal, and to repeat a line in which he had disregarded the metre. If anything were lost by the insertion of apostrophes, employed by our greatest poets in different ages, and especially warranted by Ben Jonson in his " English Grammar," the case might be different.

minor points of this description, we may adduce a passage from "The Taming of the Shrew," (act iii. sc. 2,) evidently a quotation of five short lines from a then popular ballad, which has hitherto been given as mere prose, or, at best, as an irregular couplet. It was the frequent custom of Shakespeare to make his low comic characters reply by some snatch of the kind, and the answer of Biondello, after he has been quibbling with Baptista about the arrival of Petruchio in strange apparel and on horseback, is of this kind :—

> " Nay, by Saint Jamy,
> I hold you a penny,
> A horse and a man
> Is more than one,
> And yet not many."

Some of the rhymes are licentious, but not more so than usual with scraps of ballads ; and many people, reading the lines as they are here printed, would almost be disposed to think I had made a mistake, and would turn to their Shakespeares to ascertain, if it were possible that such a passage could at any time have been printed as prose. I do not refer to these omissions as matters of much consequence, but to prove the way in which very obvious points have been neglected.

In order to render the present edition of Shake- Shakespeare complete, it is intended to include the whole speare's Poems. of his poems, which, like the plays, will be most accurately collated with the oldest and most authentic impressions. The "Venus and Adonis" will be printed from the quarto of 1593; the "Lucrece" from the quarto of 1594; the "Sonnets" from the quarto of 1609[1], and "The Passionate Pilgrim" from the octavo of 1599, compared with the reprint of 1612, omitting the poems by other authors, fraudulently inserted by the bookseller, to which it is acknowledged Shakespeare has no claim.

Manuscript authorities.

I have some new evidence of his right to the rest in a manuscript of the time to which I before referred, where the poems are inserted with Shakespeare's initials at the end; and I may take this opportunity of briefly showing how importantly this manuscript will assist us in understanding and explaining hitherto disputed passages. Take, for example, the earliest stanza in a very well-known poem: we will give it first as it stands in the old printed copy, then we will state Malone's proposed amendment, and finally, we will copy it from the manuscript to which W. S. is subscribed.

> " When as thine eye hath chose the dame,
> And stall'd the deer that thou would'st strike,
> Let reason rule things worthy blame,
> As well as fancy partial might:
> Take counsel of some wiser head,
> Neither too young, nor yet unwed."

---

[1] Nobody seems to have been aware that there are two different title-pages to the edition of Shakespeare's Sonnets in 1609; one with the imprint of William Aspley, as the bookseller who sold them, and the other with the substitution of the name of " John Wright, dwelling at Christ Church gate." —We can only guess at the reason for the change in the title-page, for there is no difference in the body of the work.

Malone discovered, from the defective rhyme, that "might" in the fourth line must be wrong, and finding "like" instead of it, in a contemporary manuscript, he altered one letter, and adopted *tike*, at the suggestion of Steevens, who, one might almost believe, was playing a trick upon his rival commentator [1]. Malone, therefore, would have the fourth line run,

> "As well as fancy, partial tike."

and so it stands in the text of the 21 vols. 8vo. Now, the manuscript before me removes the whole difficulty, and proves that a very small change indeed was necessary. We give the whole stanza from the manuscript, because there are other noticeable variations in it.

> " When that thine eye hath chose the dame,
>   And stall'd the deer that thou wouldst strike,
> Let reason rule things worthy blame,
>   As well as *partial fancy like*.
> Ask counsel of some other head,
> Neither unwise, nor yet unwed."

There cannot be a doubt that this is the true reading, and the printed copy was probably composed from a bad manuscript : the meaning of the third and fourth lines, of course, is that when a man has fixed upon a wife, he ought to let reason govern

---

[1] Malone printed it " might" in his " Supplement" 1780, vol. i. p. 726, and suggested that " wight" might possibly be the word : he afterwards adopted *tike*, in pursuance of the note by Steevens, which Malone had the simplicity to insert.

matters worthy reprehension, as well as allow partial fancy to like, or approve, his choice. This manuscript is valuable on another account, as it serves to settle Shakespeare's right to the disputed Sonnet (also to be found in Griffin's " Fidessa," 1596), commencing " Venus with Adonis sitting by her." The initials W. S. are at the end of it, independently of the fact that it is better than any other sonnet in the volume published in Griffin's name [1].

The collation of the Sonnets (many of them unquestionably autobiographical, and others possibly written for third persons, a point of considerable interest which will be duly considered in its place), and of the " Venus and Adonis," and " Lucrece," will correct many defects which have been allowed to remain in the various re-impressions of them : beautiful as the poems are, no editor seems to have

---

[1] Griffin was a gross plagiary, and nearly all that is good in the 72 sonnets contained in " Fidessa" may be traced to other authors. It has been said that Shakespeare copied his " balm of hurt minds" (Macbeth, act ii. sc. 2) from the following by Griffin, and there certainly is a resemblance :

> " Care-charmer sleep, sweet ease in restless misery,
>   The captive's liberty, and his freedom's song :
> Balm of the bruised heart, man's chief felicity,
>   Brother of quiet death, when life is too, too long."

If "Macbeth" had been written sufficiently early, (and we do not *know* that it was not) we should not have had a moment's hesitation in imputing the theft to Griffin, more particularly when we find, as is capable of distinct proof, that nearly all the rest of the quatrain above quoted is stolen from a sonnet by Daniel printed in 1592, and copied, among others, into the MS. under consideration. The coincidence between the "balm of hurt minds" of Shakespeare, and the " balm of the bruised heart" of Griffin, is worthy of remark.

thought it necessary to compare the reprints with
the originals. By way of illustration it may be
worth while to notice two or three errors in
" Lucrece." The first occurs in the short dedication
to Lord Southampton, where a word is omitted ; a
second is in the body of the poem, after Tarquin has
quitted Lucrece, and she is left to her own reflec-
tions. The original, as it is found in four copies
which I have had an opportunity of consulting, is
in these words:

> " Her house is sack'd, her quiet interrupted,
>   Her mansion batter'd by the enemy ;
>   Her sacred temple spotted, spoil'd, corrupted,
>   Grossly engirt with daring infamy," &c.

It may be asserted that the whole beauty of this
passage is absolutely ruined by the substitution of
one word for another in the third line, which in
Malone's Shakespeare by Boswell, vol. xx. p. 173,
runs thus :—

> " Her sacred *table* spotted, spoil'd, corrupted," &c.

To talk of a " table" being " spotted, spoil'd, cor-
rupted," and " grossly engirt with daring infamy" is
merely ridiculous ; and to answer that it is a misprint is no excuse, since it inevitably leads to the
corruption of all subsequent impressions, the text of
which may be taken from this supposed authentic
edition. A third instance is from nearer the con-

clusion of the poem, when Collatine and Lucrece
meet, after she has sent for him :—

> " Both stood, like old acquaintance, in a trance,
> Met far from home, wondering each other's chance."

The sense seems so plain that it is impossible to
mistake it, yet by the substitution of *but* for " both"
in the first line, the couplet is rendered something
like sheer nonsense. The blunder seems to have
been first made in 1710[1], and to have been repeated since in every reprint. It is impossible to
account for some of the perversions of the text of
which Malone (and after him Boswell) was guilty. Of
this a proof occurs early in the poem, where, in the
edition of 1594, we meet with the following couplet
at the conclusion of a stanza :—

> " And every one to rest themselves betake,
> Save thieves, and cares, and troubled minds that wake."

The first line is not strictly grammatical, but Malone,
in order to cure a slight defect in the first line, utterly
spoiled the second, and printed them thus :—

> " And every one to rest *himself betakes,*
> Save thieves and cares and troubled minds that *wakes,*"

gravely telling us, in a note, that this is the reading

---

[1] In the volume "printed for E. Curll," appended to Rowe's edition of
Shakespeare. The errors in this edition are prodigious, and not a few of
them found their way into later impressions.

of the old quarto, and that the 8vo of 1600 has "themselves betake" and "wake," when the fact is directly the reverse. He abandoned the true for a spurious reading, and by a gross mistake passed off the one for the other[1]. I make no apology for this particularity, because in my mind it relates to a point of the greatest moment, and were I disposed to try the patience of the reader I might go a great deal farther on the subject of apparently wilful alterations.

Steevens had the boldness to think and speak meanly of the minor poems of Shakespeare, and, in spite of this proof of his incompetence, the still greater boldness to comment upon his plays. Malone seems to have looked upon the minor poems rather as a necessary " supplement" to his edition, than as a part of the work on which it was worth while to bestow much labour. On the other hand, I venture to think, that Shakespeare's genius never shone forth with more intense brilliancy, his fancy never

---

[1] Since this observation was originally printed, I have taken an opportunity of visiting Oxford for the purpose of examining Malone's copy of the " Lucrece " of 1594, that I might ascertain whether there was any variation between that and the four other copies I have had the means of inspecting. To my surprise, I found that Malone's copy supports his reading, while those of the Duke of Devonshire, the late Mr. Caldecott, and two others, contradict it. The same remark will apply to the word " apologies " in the fifth stanza of " Lucrece," which in Malone's copy of 1594 is printed in the singular ; but no such excuse can be made for errors in other cases. This difference, never hitherto suspected, between copies of the same edition is remarkable, and shows that it is impossible to collate too many of them. The corrections must have been made as the poem passed through the press, and they tend to confirm the opinion that Shakespeare himself superintended the publication of his earlier works.

sported with more playful vigour, and the philosophy of his mind never displayed its depth and power more remarkably than in these productions: if he had left nothing else behind him, he would have merited to be placed among the first and greatest poets of the world.

Notes to the new Edition.

Having stated all that I consider immediately necessary regarding the text of the projected edition of the Works of Shakespeare, it remains to say a few words of the notes which will accompany that text. The first care will be to make those notes as few and as concise as possible, so that the attention of the reader is diverted from the author as rarely and as briefly as is consistent with a clear understanding of his words. The multiplication of notes, first committing a blunder, and then endeavouring to correct it, is a most inconvenient evil attending the perusal of many of the editions of Shakespeare, and has often led the admirers of his writings to wish that they had never sustained the misfortune of comment and illustration. The method an editor ought to pursue is clearly this:— to settle the true reading; then, to form an accurate judgment whether that reading is intelligible; and thirdly, if a note be required, to say no more than is necessary. On these plain principles I have endeavoured to proceed. Information upon temporary allusions, obsolete customs, and peculiar manners, will at times be wanted, but here also brevity and clearness will be studied.

The insertion of what are called parallel passages (frequently rather at right angles than parallel) will usually be avoided altogether, and will never be resorted to for the display of what Lord Bacon terms " vain learning." If the resemblance be strong and striking, and the meaning of Shakespeare thereby explained and illustrated, they may now and then be useful. I shall never avail myself of the assistance of predecessors without due acknowledgment, but the repetition of names at the conclusion of unimportant notes rather tends to confuse than to inform. The great purpose ought to be to permit the author to speak for himself : he usually speaks very intelligibly, and rarely needs any aid, excepting where some corruption of the text may be established or suspected.

The introductory matter to each play will commonly be entirely new. Much information respecting the origin of Shakespeare's plots, as well as the performance of his dramas, has been acquired since the publication of Malone's edition by Boswell, and it will be carefully collected, properly arranged, and placed perspicuously, but compendiously, before the reader, in order that he may be deficient in no point of knowledge, and that whenever a doubt arises, he may refer with confidence to our projected edition for the removal of it. *Introductions to the plays.*

Of late years a much wider range and more intellectual system of criticism upon Shakespeare has *Criticisms on Shakespeare.*

been introduced; and at the head of this class of commentators on his spirit and poetry may be placed our countryman Coleridge. To a series of his Lectures on the productions of our great dramatist I first listened more than twenty years ago, taking and preserving notes of all that fell from him. Much depended with him upon the impulse of the moment, and what has been published since his death, sometimes gives but an outline of his thoughts and of the manner in which they were expressed. Of these I shall not omit to avail myself. What may have been well and justly said by German critics, especially by such men as Tieck and Schlegel, will also be brought under the reader's notice, taking care, however, not to obtrude the rhapsodical outpourings of their extravagant and ignorant imitators, whether abroad or at home.

Chronological Order.

This may be said to bring us to the point, in what succession the plays will be printed in our edition. Malone, Chalmers, Drake, and Dyce [1], have all offered tables of the " chronological order " in which they suppose Shakespeare wrote his various productions for the stage, but it is singular how rarely they agree; and although I have before me highly important materials for the purpose, with which my predecessors were unacquainted, I confess my inability to settle more than a few points satisfac-

[1] See the Aldine edition of Shakespeare's Poems, 12mo, 1832. The " Chronology" is appended to a short but excellent " Memoir" of the Poet.

torily. Let us take an instance, proving the uncertainty that attends such speculations.—" Twelfth Night." Tyrwhitt was of opinion that this comedy was not written until 1614, and Malone for some years thought so too ; but he afterwards entirely altered his mind, and came to the conclusion, for various reasons which he assigns at large, that " Twelfth Night" was written in 1607. What is the fact? That at whatever period it came from the pen of Shakespeare, it was certainly acted at the Middle Temple Feast on the 2nd February, 1602. This is indisputable, (vide History of English Dramatic Poetry and the Stage, vol. i. p. 327,) and it shows in the strongest light the utter futility of such conjectures.

There are, it is true, some leading facts upon this question, which do not admit of dispute. In 1598, as most readers of Shakespeare are aware, Francis Meres published his *Palladis Tamia*[1], which con-

Meres' *Palladis Tamia*.

---

[1] In the Bibliographical and Critical Catalogue of the Library at Bridgewater House, (privately printed for Lord Francis Egerton, 4to, 1837) I suggested that Meres might possibly be the author of the anonymous collection of Epigrams and Satires published in 1598, under the title of " Skialetheia, or a Shadow of Truth," 8vo. I have since discovered that the name of the writer of that work is Edward Guilpin, who is known to bibliographers, by some commendatory verses before Markham's " Devereux," 1597, &c. The fact is, that " England's Parnassus," 8vo, 1600, contains a variety of quotations subscribed " Edw. Guilpin," and all these are contained in " Skialetheia." There cannot, therefore, be any doubt that " Skialetheia " was his authorship. It contains much that is illustrative of the opinions, manners, and literature of the latter end of the reign of Elizabeth, and particular notices of Sidney, Spenser, Daniel, Drayton, Marston, Hall, &c. It is a work of extreme rarity as

tains a list of some of Shakespeare's plays, then known either because they had been printed or acted: we shall insert the titles exactly as we find them in the work of Meres (Sign. O o 2), and in the order in which he places them.

"Gentlemen of Verona."
"Errors."
"Love Labours Lost."
"Love Labours Won."
"Midsummer Night Dream."
"Merchant of Venice."
"Richard the II."
"Richard the III."
"Henry the IV."
"King John."
"Titus Andronicus."
"Romeo and Juliet."

It is supposed that "Love Labours Won" is not a lost drama, but "All's Well that ends Well" under a different title; the Rev. Joseph Hunter, in his acute and learned "Dissertation on the Tempest," contends that that drama, and not "All's Well that ends Well," is the "Love Labours Won" of Meres; but I do not concur in his view, though supported with ingenuity, among others, for a reason which will appear presently. Including "Love Labours Won," Meres only supplies a list of about a third of the existing dramas of Shakespeare; yet he (who

well as interest, and it is to be hoped that it may soon be re-printed by one of our Literary Societies. A copy of it is preserved among Malone's books at Oxford.

was evidently well acquainted with our plays and poetry,) does not speak as if he had omitted any play produced before he published his *Palladis Tamia*[1]. He does not furnish us with the slightest means of knowing in what order these twelve (or thirteen, if we suppose that Meres includes both parts of "Henry IV.") dramas appeared, unless we are to take it that he meant to enumerate them in that order. Therefore, although we are thus aware that they were known in 1598 as works by Shakespeare, we are still ignorant of the precise dates when they were produced.

There is another authority with reference to some "England's Parnassus." of these plays, which has never before been adduced. In 1600 came out "England's Parnassus," an octavo volume of more than 500 pages of extracts from plays and poems by various authors, and among them there are nearly 100 quotations to which the name or initials of Shakespeare are appended. Some blunders are certainly committed in these ascriptions, such as attributing a well-remembered passage in

[1] Meres makes no mention of "Henry VI.," although there is good ground for supposing that all the three parts under that title were among the earliest pieces from the pen of Shakespeare. "The Taming of the Shrew" had likewise, in all probability, been produced either in or soon after 1594, when the older "Taming of a Shrew" was published, perhaps in consequence of the success at the theatre of Shakespeare's improvement upon that story : nevertheless, Meres omits it, and hence an inference may possibly be drawn, that he did not include "Henry VI." nor "The Taming of the Shrew" among Shakespeare's plays, because our great dramatist was not alone concerned in the authorship of them.

"Richard II." to Drayton [1], and two lines in the "Fairy Queen" to Shakespeare, but in general they are correct. Most of the extracts are from "Venus and Adonis" and "Lucrece," but others are from plays; and it is somewhat remarkable that no play is there quoted, that is not to be found in the list given by Meres. The plays are not named in "England's Parnassus," but by tracing the quotations I find them to be these :—

"Love's Labours Lost" (quoted twice).
"Henry IV. Part I." (quoted twice).
"Richard II." (quoted five times).
"Richard III." (quoted five times).
"Romeo and Juliet" (quoted eleven times).

So that our list of extant plays in 1598, is not increased by the quotations made from them up to the year 1600. Hence we might possibly infer that between the publication of *Palladis Tamia*, in 1598, and of "England's Parnassus," in 1600, Shakespeare had not added to his stock of dramas. Possibly, too, as "Henry IV. Part II." is not cited in "England's Parnassus," it had not been brought out as early in 1600 as "England's Parnassus" came from the press, and Meres, in 1598, might only allude to the first part of that historical drama.

[1] When Mr. T. Park reprinted "England's Parnassus" in "Heliconia," (3 vols. 4to, 1815,) he did not detect, or at all events did not point out, the mistake. He seems to have fancied that,

"This royal throne of kings, this sceptred isle,
This earth of majesty, this seat of Mars," &c.

were lines by Michael Drayton.

With respect to two other plays, "Twelfth Night" and "Othello," we have distinct evidence that they were acted in 1602; the first, as already mentioned, at the Middle Temple, in February, and the second at Lord Keeper Egerton's, at Harefield, in August. The latter circumstance is stated in my "New Particulars respecting Shakespeare and his Works," p. 58, on the authority of MS. family accounts preserved at Bridgewater House. In the same tract the "Note-Book" of Dr. Forman is adduced, to prove that the four following plays were acted at the dates affixed to them.

"Macbeth"	20th April, 1610.
"Cymbeline" . . .	in 1610 or 1611.
"Richard II." [1] . . .	30th April, 1611.
"Winter's Tale" . .	15th May, 1611.

We have only spoken of seventeen, or, at most, eighteen plays, and these are all the dates that have hitherto been positively ascertained respecting the writing or acting of any of them; excepting, of course, as far as the printing of particular dramas affords proof that they had been previously brought upon the stage. I now come to some very interesting and decisive evidence with regard to others, which has only been brought to light within the last

New evidence on the chronology.

---

[1] In "New Particulars," &c. reasons are given for thinking that this was another play on the events of the reign of Richard II., not the work of Shakespeare. Mr. Amyot suggested, and argued with great ingenuity, that it was possibly a *first part* of "Richard II.," which Shakespeare may have written, but which has not come down to us. (See his Letter upon this point in "New Particulars," &c. p. 16.)

few months. The precise nature of it, and the depository where it was discovered, will be stated in detail in the introductions to the plays themselves, when we come to print them: in the meantime I may mention, that I shall be able to show most indisputably, that the subsequent plays by Shakespeare, his name being given in connection with the titles, were represented at court at the dates hereunder specified :—

"Othello," performed on the 1st Nov. 1604.
"The Merry Wives of Windsor," performed on the Sunday after Nov. 1, 1604.
"Measure for Measure," performed on St. Stephen's Night, 1604.
"The Comedy of Errors," performed on Innocents' Night, 1604.
"Love's Labours Lost," performed between the 1st and 6th January, 1605.
"Henry the Fifth," performed on the 7th January, 1605.
"The Merchant of Venice," performed on Shrove-Sunday, and again on Shrove-Tuesday, 1605.
"The Winter's Tale," performed on the 5th November, 1611.
"The Tempest," performed on Hallowmas Night, 1611.

This evidence, unknown to those who have hitherto written on the works and life of Shakespeare, establishes in the first place that some of his earliest pieces were performed at court as late as 1604 and 1605, such as his " Comedy of Errors," " Love's Labours Lost," and " Merchant of Venice," all three of which, as we have seen on the authority of Meres, had been produced before 1598. " The Merchant of Venice" was so much liked by the king in 1605, that having been first played on

Shrove-Sunday, it was repeated " by command " the next day but one. Othello, we have shown, was in existence more than two years anterior to Nov. 1604. It is supposed by Malone, that " Henry V." may have been written in 1599, " The Merry Wives of Windsor" in 1601, and " Measure for Measure" in 1603 : the last might therefore be nearly a new play on St. Stephen's night, 1604; but the two first could hardly have been recommended for performance at court, by the fact that they were enjoying their first run of popularity at a public theatre. It seems probable that " The Winter's Tale," and " The Tempest," were sufficient novelties, and sufficient favourites with the public in 1611, to be selected on this account. Forman had seen " The Winter's Tale" at the Globe Theatre on the 15th May preceding the performance of it at court, and Malone was of opinion that " The Tempest" was a new play in 1611. Under the uncertainty attending this part of the subject, it may however be urged, that not one of the nine plays above enumerated was chosen for representation at court, because it was new and popular. James I. had not been long on the throne in 1605, and had not, therefore, seen many of the older plays which had been acted before Queen Elizabeth : the case was somewhat different in 1611, and then the old custom of selecting plays for performance at court, which were suggested by their success at the public theatres, might be revived, because the king had by that time seen most of the old stock-plays.

What, then, is the conclusion at which I am disposed to arrive, founded upon the preceding information?—that although we have at present many lights
upon the question of chronology, which formerly did
not exist, yet we cannot even now make more than
a plausible conjecture as to the earliest dates of most
of Shakespeare's plays. In thirteen instances we
know when they were performed, but not whether
they were then performed for the first time, so that
no criterion as to the period when they were written
can well be more uncertain. I once thought that
Henslowe's MS. Diary might afford some clue to
guide us. Under the years 1594 and 1595 we
there meet with the following names of plays, which
resemble the titles of some of Shakespeare's known
or imputed works—" Hamlet,"—" The Taming of a
Shrew,"—" Andronicus,"—" The Venetian Comedy,"
—" Palamon and Arcite,"—" Cæsar and Pompey,"—
" Antony and Vallea,"—" The second part of Cæsar,"
—" Harry the 5th," and " Troy;" but with respect
to some of them, there is good reason to believe that
they were old plays upon subjects Shakespeare afterwards adopted, and we may be disposed to presume
the same of the rest. Upon this point, nevertheless,
we may be entirely mistaken. Under the date of
22nd May, 1602, we learn on similar authority, that
Webster, Middleton, and other poets were engaged
in writing a tragedy called " Cæsar's Fall," (not
noticed by Malone,) and that in September of the
same year Henry Chettle was preparing a comedy

Henslowe's Diary.

under the title of "Robin Good-fellow" (also omitted
by Malone); and we might infer that Webster and
his play-partners, as well as Chettle, were induced
to take up these subjects, either by the success of
"Julius Cæsar," and "Midsummer Night's Dream,"
or by hearing that Shakespeare was employed upon
them; but with respect to the last, we know that it
was in existence in 1598. Malone discovered in
Henslowe's Diary several entries regarding a "Troilus
and Cressida," by Dekker and Chettle, in April 1599;
but we do not know that those dramatists were not
then composing additions or alterations to Shakespeare's play with the same title, or they might even
be writing a rival play, to compete with that by
Shakespeare. All these must continue mere matters of speculation, especially when we find that in
June 1602 Ben Jonson was preparing a historical
drama upon the events of the reign of Richard III.,
although Shakespeare had written a play upon the
same subject, which was printed five years before,
and which long continued, as we have every reason
to believe, extremely popular.

As to about half the dramas of our great dramatist, Order of
printing
we are totally destitute of anything approaching the plays.
distinct information when they were first acted,
much more when they were first written. Of
six and thirty plays, only seventeen were published
during Shakespeare's life: "Othello" came from the
press in 1622; and the rest (with the exception
of "Pericles,") were printed for the first time in

the folio of 1623. "Pericles," printed in quarto in 1609, was not inserted in that edition, for reasons to be assigned when I come to speak separately of that drama. The folio of 1623 was arranged, as far as we can now ascertain, by Heminge and Condell, Shakespeare's fellow-actors, who doubtless had performed in most of the plays, which are inserted in the volume under the three heads of " Comedies," " Histories," and " Tragedies." The player-editors were, most likely, generally, if not particularly acquainted with the periods when the pieces were originally produced on the stage, yet they obviously made no arrangement as to dates; and under the uncertainty which must unavoidably belong to any conjectural classification of the kind, I have thought that we could not do better than adopt the course pursued in 1623, so near to the time when Shakespeare was living, and when the matter must have been fresh in the recollection of many [1]. Any opinion depending upon a comparison

---

[1] Each division of " Comedies," " Histories," and " Tragedies," is separately paged in the folio of 1623. The " Comedies" occupy 303 pages, the back of p. 303 being left blank. The " Histories" fill 232 pages, after which follows " Troilus and Cressida," which is unpaged, excepting that the second leaf is marked 79 and 80. In the " Tragedies," the last page appears to be 993, but this is a misprint for 393, and in the course of this portion of the volume an error of 100 pages is committed, 156 being followed by 257, and so on to the end. From the circumstances that " Troilus and Cressida " is unpaged, and that the title is not found in the " Catalogue " at the commencement of the volume, it has been supposed that it was originally omitted, and was added to the collection as an after-thought ; but the work obviously went through the hands of more than one printer, and in this way the mistake might have been occasioned, without supposing

of the earlier with the later style of Shakespeare, the reader will be able to form for himself, and all the ascertained facts, which may serve to aid him in any inquiry of the kind, will be carefully given at the commencement of each play [1].

The biography of Shakespeare, and the relations subsisting between him and his contemporaries, will form an important portion of our first volume. In order to render it as complete and perfect as possible, I shall resort to no second-hand authorities, but shall examine the original sources of information, from the register of his baptism to the proof of his will. Of late years, and even within the last few months, many new facts, of great interest with reference to Shakespeare's life and residence in London, have been brought to light; and we shall of course take care that none of them, however minute, are omitted. Some points of the history of our great dramatist

Life of Shakespeare.

Heminge and Condell ignorant of the fact, that "Troilus and Cressida," printed in 1609 with Shakespeare's name on the title-page, ought to be included. The name of the author was not printed on any of the early editions of "Romeo and Juliet." I allude to the impressions published in the years 1597, 1599, and 1609.

[1] Malone sometimes adopted a very loose mode of reasoning when he wanted to establish a point. He wished to show that "Henry V." was produced by the poet in 1598, and he found two lines in Daniel's "Civil Wars," printed in 1595, which strongly resemble a passage in "Henry V. :" hence he concluded that the play was not written before 1596, as Shakespeare could not earlier have borrowed from Daniel. But Daniel was much more likely to borrow from Shakespeare, than Shakespeare from Daniel ; and if Daniel did borrow two lines from Shakespeare's "Henry V." it must have been written before Daniel published his "Civil Wars" in 1595. I only adduce this circumstance as a proof how little reliance is to be placed upon conjectures so supported.

must still rest upon reasoning and conjecture, but not a few particulars, which in the time of Malone were mere matters of speculation, have since been distinctly ascertained. Although Malone went on, nearly to the day of his death, collecting such materials as he could procure, he never (as far as any printed evidence remains to us) was able to add anything important to his previous stock of information, and expired, leaving the biography of Shakespeare to be completed by Boswell, from the scattered papers which devolved into his hands.

The " Memoirs of Edward Alleyn," the contemporary of our great dramatist, recently printed for the Shakespeare Society, supply evidence that Malone did not make use of much curious information long in his hands, derived from original papers formerly belonging to the actor-founder of Dulwich College ; and it may be stated with confidence, that more particulars for an accurate biography of Shakespeare have been procured since the death of Malone, than he was able to accumulate. We have now the exact date of the bond given anterior to his marriage in 1582 : and although we cannot positively fix the year of his arrival in London, we can show that he had risen to considerable eminence in his profession as early as 1589. In 1592 we find him exciting the jealousy of rival dramatists, and in 1596 a very prominent member of the company acting at the Black-friars Theatre, continuing to advance in rank and importance in connexion with the stage, until, at the

accession of James I., he was one of the leaders of
the company which the king took into his pay and
employment. Thus we are able to trace his progress
to the year 1604, the latest date at which his name
is any where introduced as an actor, and about which
time he no doubt quitted the stage. He occupied a
good house in Southwark in 1608, and his final re-
tirement from London to his native town may now
be stated with more certainty than ever to have
occurred in 1612. In April of that year Edward
Alleyn became the purchaser of considerable property in the precinct of the Blackfriars, including
either the whole or a large share of the theatre, and
there is sufficient ground for believing that this had
been the property of Shakespeare, and that he disposed of it to Alleyn just before he withdrew to
Stratford, and ceased to have any connexion with
dramatic affairs in the metropolis or elsewhere. We
shall also be able to show in satisfactory detail his
gradual acquisition of wealth, and the public and
private patronage he enjoyed.

In order that nothing may be wanting to the com- Origin of
pleteness of the undertaking, I shall introduce the our stage
and drama.
biography of our great poet by a succinct history
of the origin, rise, and progress of dramatic perform-
ances in this country, that every reader may be
acquainted with the precise condition of our stage
and its poetry, at the time when Shakespeare first
became connected with it. This part of the subject
will necessarily embrace notices of his immediate

predecessors and contemporaries, regarding whom I shall have to offer much that will be new and interesting to the philologist, the antiquary, and the general reader. The object is to include in eight volumes octavo as faultless a text of Shakespeare's plays and poems as can be established, accompanied by everything necessary to a full understanding of his works, and a just estimate of his character.

In conclusion I may, perhaps, be permitted to state, that it was the intention of some members of the Council of the Shakespeare Society to recommend that an edition of the Works of our great dramatist should be issued under the sanction of that body; but as soon as they learnt that a proposal of the kind had been made to me, they most handsomely relinquished their design. They knew during how many years I had been preparing such a publication, and they were willing to believe that to allow me to proceed with it would accomplish, in several important respects, the object they had in view. They, and other literary and antiquarian friends, have likewise promptly tendered such assistance as cannot fail to be most valuable in completing the undertaking. With the individual responsibility attending it, I am, nevertheless, most deeply impressed.

THE END.